DORE TOTLEY AND BEYOND

THE DRAWINGS OF BRIAN EDWARDS

SHEFFIELD 7 MILES

VIEW TOWARDS SHEFFIELD FROM OWLER BAR 1989 BRIAN EDWARDS.

ACKNOWLEDGEMENTS

I would like to thank, once again, local residents too numerous to mention, for their continued snippets of information, loan of photographs and general encouragement.

May I also thank the past and present editors of the Totley Independent and also those contributors who have maintained this useful source of local history and current information for so many years. In more recent times *'Dore to Door'* magazine has equally been of tremendous importance to the local community. I urge all readers to send letters, articles and illustrations to these local non-profit making publications.

I also owe thanks to those residents who have allowed me to sketch their premises.

Many years ago Dore and Totley were part of the parish of Dronfield and I am pleased that the printers of this book are located there. Walker and Carson have again been superb, always patient and helpful, allowing me to overshoot deadlines.

Local shops are to be thanked for selling publications over the years and several Sheffield and Derbyshire booksellers have been most supportive. Lastly I would like to thank my wife Pam for putting up with my early morning and late night shuffling back and forward to the drawing board, for her constructive comments and typing skill and just being my wife.

The Author

Brian Edwards Born Manchester 1937 now lives in Great Longstone, Derbyshire.

Educated Manchester Grammar School, King Edward VII School in Sheffield, Certificate in Architecture University of Sheffield, Certificate in local History Sheffield Hallam University, member of the Society of Architectural Illustrators, Worked in architectural and design offices U.K. and Switzerland. Joint founder of Shape Design in 1967 and has worked as interior designer to local, national and international organisations. He has recently taken early retirement to concentrate on publishing and illustration.

Interests: family and work, walking, running, skiing, cycling, drawing, photography, painting, local history and travel.

Illustrations in various publications including the Morning Telegraph.

Previous books:
Drawings of Historic Totley
The Totley Tunnel
Sheffield and the Peak

DORE, TOTLEY AND BEYOND

Introduction

Dore and Totley are ancient settlements with the former's fame going back to the meeting between Kings Ecgbert and Eanred in 829 AD. Both places are included in the Domesday survey of 1086 AD.

However there is evidence of early man dating back at least 3000 years; various finds on the moors above Totley can be seen in Sheffield Museum.

Until 1935, the boundary between Derbyshire and Yorkshire followed the Limb Brook which tumbles down through Ecclesall Woods.

Since both villages were absorbed into the city of Sheffield their populations have increased considerably and these days the fringes overlap. Gone are the days of two isolated settlements one and a half miles apart, but the Old Hay valley is preserved as a green corridor passing between both and extending up the moors. Thus there are dozens of rural footpaths and bridleways leading alongside and across streams.

Both villages retain a character of their own with many interesting old buildings.

Since 1978 when we launched the Totley Independent I have spent many hours recording the area and perhaps over two hundred sketches have appeared in both the 'INDY' and the 'Dore to Door' magazines. In addition I have published two books 'Drawings of Historic Totley' and 'Totley and the Tunnel', both of which are now out of print.

'Dore Totley and Beyond' puts together illustrations both published and unpublished before, many having been drawn in the last year..

I haven't yet exhausted my supply of illustrations and such is the variety and interest of the area that there are many more subjects waiting to be drawn. Therefore I hope to be able to furnish both local magazines for years to come. By the time you read this book I will have taken early retirement from Shape Design and begun a new career concentrating on publishing and illustration. For the first time I will be able to devote more working hours to my interests.

I hope that you enjoy looking through this book and trust that some sketches will evoke happy memories for you.

Brian Edwards
Great Longstone

OWLER BAR BRIAN EDWARDS 1990.

THE RIVER SHEAF BELOW TOTLEY RISE
NOV. 1991 BRIAN EDWARDS.

The River Sheaf is fed here by two main
tributaries. The Totley Brook forms the boundary between
Totley and Holmesfield whilst the Old Hay Brook
separates Dore from Totley. Just below the point at Totley
Rise where the two meet is this weir. The diverted water
fed two long-vanished water mills – Bradway Mill and
Upper Wheel.

Dore Village Green is a fine space surrounded by mature trees and several old buildings. It is the venue for the Annual Well Dressing.

The Old School built in 1821 on the site of a previous school. On the right hand side is the section originally housing the teacher; from 1821 to 1848 Richard Furness was installed here. When Dore's new school was built nearby, the old building was renovated for community use.

The Green is a convenient and pleasant place for scholars to enjoy a picnic lunch.

In 1932 Dore Parish Council erected a memorial to local men who lost their lives in the First World War. A stone nearby commemorates the Crimean War and is inscribed Peace 1856.

This stone on the Village Green commemorates the 829 AD Treaty of Dore when King Ecgbert, conqueror of the centre and the south of England, was 'offered obedience' by the Eanred of Northumbria.

One of the older buildings fronting onto the Village Green is Sycamore Cottage.

DORE OLD SCHOOL 1995
BRIAN EDWARDS.

SYCAMORE COTTAGE,
DORE VILLAGE GREEN TOPSIDE 1995
BRIAN EDWARDS.

WAR MEMORIAL
DORE 1995
BRIAN EDWARDS.

DORE VILLAGE GREEN
COMMEMORATIVE STONE 1995 BRIAN EDWARDS.

BRIAN
EDWARDS

DORE VILLAGE
GREEN 1981.

BEAUCHIEF ABBEY BRIAN EDWARDS 1995.

Beauchief Abbey stands in a semi-rural setting although partly surrounded by the golf course. Built in 1183 by the canons who had mills on the River Sheaf and had a sheep grange up on Strawberry Lee. Today the carp ponds provide an idyllic spot for local anglers and the walk from here up to Bradway passes near Beauchief Hall..

page 8

Beauchief Abbey farm was built around 1700, but has had later additions. To this day the area around the farm retains a rural character and the old ponds which supplied the monks with their diet of carp still remain. The Round Walk passes nearby before passing through Ladies Spring Wood and emerging onto Twentywell Lane near Dore Station.

The woods on Bradway Bank are a delight with occasional views through the oak trees of Dore and Abbeydale. This path leading from Totley Rise eventually skirts around above the Bradway Tunnel, past the now-defunct Twentywell Brickyard and emerges by the Castle Inn.

OAKS ON BRADWAY BANK   BRIAN EDWARDS 1996.

The path on the previous page rises through Poynton Wood on its way up from Totley Rise passing the flat development which replaced West View Cottage, formerly an old mill building.

There is reason to think that the path from Twentywell through Poynton Wood crossed the Totley Brook at Totley Rise and continued up Akley Bank near the Methodist Church.

Before the Heatherfield Estate (Marstone, Stonecroft etc.) was developed (1911) there was a path leading up Akley towards Totley.

FOOTPATH THROUGH
POYNTON WOOD
BRIAN EDWARDS 1995.

AKLEY BANK
TOTLEY RISE
BRIAN EDWARDS 1990.

A view from Hathersage Road across Dore catches a glimpse of Beauchief Abbey in the background with the Dore Moor House roofs clearly visible in front. After Johnson Firth Brown stopped using it as a company guest house in 1984, it was sold and split into 10 lots.

As I write, the Dam to Abbeydale Works has been drained to facilitate repairs to the dam wall. The adjoining Beauchief Gardens and the dam were presented in 1935 to the City of Sheffield by the J. G. Graves Charitable Trust.

BEAUCHIEF DAM   BRIAN EDWARDS 1996

Abbeydale Industrial Hamlet is a favourite lunch time place for me. It's a good place for a snack, cosy in winter and al fresco in warmer weather. One other plus is that the museum shop sells local publications (including this one).

ABBEYDALE INDUSTRIAL HAMLET   BRIAN EDWARDS '96

OLDHAY TOTLEY
BRIAN EDWARDS 1990

19. The oasis of calm known as Old
Hay belies the noisy and dirty activity
that filled this Hamlet between the
16th and 19th centuries. For this was
the site of a lead mill and the clear,
gurgling Old Hay Brook passing
under the old stone bridge today was
once a lethal cocktail of poisonous
lead. Hard to imagine.

BRIDGE AT OLD HAY
TOTLEY
BRIAN EDWARDS
1990

NEEDHAMS DIKE NEAR TOTLEY GROVE BRIAN EDWARDS 1990

COTTAGES AT OLD HAY TOTLEY BRIAN EDWARDS 1990.

These semi detached brick houses here were no doubt built in the last century to house the mill workers. Recently, extensive alterations transformed them to a substantial stone-built house.

The Old Hay lead mill dam alongside the Old Hay Brook is now an attractive lawn with only part of the old stone shuttle visible.

Further downstream a corn mill, later Upper Mill Scythe Works, was fed by the brook and the Needhams Dike which followed Penny Lane and emerged as it does today through this tunnel into Old Hay Brook.

THE OLD LEAD MILL DAM AT OLDHAY TOTLEY BRIAN EDWARDS 1990.

THE OLD CORN MILL DAM FIELD TOTLEY 1996. BRIAN EDWARDS.

These days only the line of old trees, in the field
adjoining Hillfoot Road, pick out the line of the
old Corn Mill dam.

THOMPSONS FARM
BACK LANE TOTLEY RISE
BRIAN EDWARDS 1990.

Another dam was that for Totley Rolling Mill located to the rear of the later Totley Rise shops. Presently a pleasant piece of grazing land bordered by the Totley Brook. It housed, until last year, agricultural building, sometimes known as Thompsons Farm after the local butcher/farmer. It was sadly demolished after vandalism led to a fire.

At the lower end of the dam stood, and still stands, the stone-built mill managers house and the row of mill workers cottages.

MILL LANE TOTLEY RISE WITH
THE ROLLING MILL COTTAGES
NOV. 1991 BRIAN EDWARDS.

The site of the old dam can be seen from the narrow back lane
behind Totley Rise shops and possibly under threat from a new
housing development.

BRIAN EDWARDS   BACK LANE TOTLEY RISE 1996.

MILLDALE ROAD TOTLEY RISE C1965
BRIAN EDWARDS 1996.

Milldale Road houses follow the edge of the Rolling Mill
dam wall. The stones were taken to Millhouses for the
Wagon and Horses extension. Bradway Bank can be seen in
the background.

COTTAGES ON STRAWBERRY DEE LANE, TOTLEY BENTS   BRIAN EDWARDS 1995

CURVED WALL, TOTLEY BENTS 1975 BRIAN EDWARDS 1995

It is quite likely that at the opposite end of Totley, nestling under the moors, these cottages were home to mill workers, probably grinders at the nearby Totley Forge. The men would work the wheels in the winter when water was more abundant and then turn to agriculture in the summer. Some of the cottages have been converted to a single house.

BENTS FARM, TOTLEY BENTS   BRIAN EDWARDS 1996.   658

Nearby at Totley Bents stands one of several working farms in the area. It's buildings became a doss house in the 1880's for the workers in the Totley Tunnel. Later the Grouse Inn was opened in an adjacent building.

Monnybrook is another hamlet close to Totley Bents. In the 1980's these three cottages were altered to provide a single dwelling house. Immediately behind is the Totley Rifle Range opened in 1900. Monny Brook is local dialect for many brooks.

COTTAGES AT MONNY BROOK 1960s BRIAN EDWARDS 83

page 21

MOSS ROAD

MONNYBROOKS
TOTLEY FEBRUARY
BRIAN EDWARDS 1990.

LANE HEAD ROAD

PENNY LANE
TOTLEY 1990
BRIAN EDWARDS

Bank View farm is another building in Monnybrook standing at the corner of Moss Road which ascends up towards Totley Moor..

Further along Lane Head Road, is the recreation ground, scene of many tussles in the tough Derbyshire Leagues. The wood in the centre of this view cloaks the huge tip of waste dug out of the nearby Totley railway tunnel.

Penny Lane with the wooded waste tip to the left and the small stream called Needhams Dike on the opposite side. This stream rises out of a spring high above behind the brickyards.

HILLFOOT ROAD
TOTLEY 1996   BRIAN EDWARDS

Hillfoot is the area at the junction of Hillfoot Road and
Penny Lane. As long ago as the 1500's it was called
Bentley with several more buildings. At one time the lane
ran through a ford near here.

FOOTPATH UP FISHERS MOOR TOTLEY   BRIAN EDWARDS 1995

THE RESERVE DAM TOTLEY FORGE
BRIAN EDWARDS 1996.

Down at Hallfield time seems to have stood still. A path runs down from Strawberry Lee Lane, across Fishers Moor, pitted with mine shafts, and crosses the Lee Dike which enters the Old Hay Brook at what we call (the now grassed over) reserve dam feeding Totley Forge. In the 17th century there was a paper mill downstream.

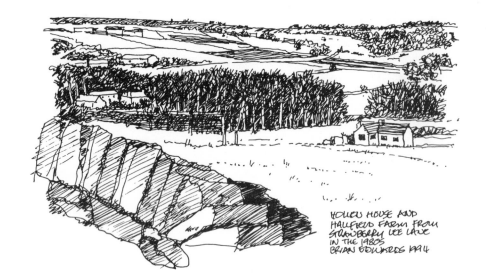

At the lower end of the dam stood, and still stand, the stone built mill managers house and the row of mill workers cottages.

HOLLOW HOUSE AND
HALLFIELD FARM FROM
STRAWBERRY LEE LANE
IN THE 1980s
BRIAN EDWARDS 1994

Hallfield Farm nestling in the trees, Hollen House in the foreground and Houndkirk Moor on the horizon.

This view over the Shorts Lane area from Newfield Lane, shows the strip of agricultural land between Dore and the moors. The highest hill in the background is called Wimbleholme and the old sheepgrange at Strawberry Lee was located in the dip to the right.

VIEW OVER SHORTS LANE DORE. BRIAN EDWARDS 1995

STOOPS NEAR
HALLFIELD FARM BRIAN EDWARDS '95

HALLFIELD FARM 1996 BRIAN EDWARDS.

Hallfield Farm can be glimpsed
from the footpath which crosses
two bridges and squeezes
between several sets of gritstone
stoops.

Totley Hall was built by George Newbould in 1623 although there home had been an earlier building on the site.

The buildings were altered and extended between 1883 and 1892. Sheffield Corporation bought Totley Hall in 1949 for £5850 and established a college of further education. It is now part of Sheffield Hallam University.

TOTLEY HALL 1980 BRIAN EDWARDS

Church Lane Farm in Dore from the rear before it was altered. Most people would d agree that the work was carried our sympathetically and the result has matured even further to enhance the area. This part of the road was renamed Vicarage Lane.

A number of old buildings still stand much as they were 200 years or more ago. The cottage with its gable end to the lane was built by Anthony Woodhouse in 1704. Nowadays this is called Hillfoot Road and leads down from Baslow Road towards Dore. In the 1840's it was known as Town Road or Dore Road.

HILLFOOT ROAD TOTLEY
BRIAN EDWARDS 1990

Woodbine Cottage on Vicarage Lane, Dore was built in the seventeenth century and is thought to have replaced an earlier building. The cottage has been extended and altered and some old features removed but more recently it has been part restored. There are several other old buildings on this stretch of Vicarage Lane.

WOODBINE COTTAGE VICARAGE LANE DORE   BRIAN EDWARDS 1996

VICARAGE LANE, DORE   BRIAN EDWARDS 1996

CANNON HALL 1979
TOTLEY
BRIAN EDWARDS

Cannon Hall thought by some to be the oldest surviving building in the district – the part to the right has a cruck construction with the gable added much later. Cannon Hall is tucked away on Butts Hill near All Saints School, Totley.

Shrewsbury Terrace is a fine row of stone built cottages adjacent to Cannon Hall. They were built in the last century and are said to have had file grinders workshops to the rear.

6 SHREWSBURY TERRACE IN 1981
BRIAN EDWARDS 1995.
UP FOR AUCTION

HALL LANE FARM IN TOTLEY HALL LANE.

It is always good to see working farms in the centre of villages. Totley Hall Lane had several more at one time and there is pressure to reduce the viability of Hall Lane farm by using part of the land for houses. Don't do it!

Next door is Totley Hall Farm, no doubt once serving the hall. The present occupants have established a fair sized fruit farm on the fields bordering the ancient Gillfield Wood.

1994 TOTLEY HALL FARM BRIAN EDWARDS

TOTLEY HALL FARM 1995 BRIAN EDWARDS
FROM LOWFIELDS.

Old cottages and farms are tucked away like Rose Cottage on Ash House Lane or exposed to the extremes of the weather such as the recently refurbished Roundseats Farm on Whitelow Lane.

COTTAGE IN LIMB LANE DORE   BRIANEDWARDS 1996

VIEW FROM SHORTS LANE DORE 1995. BRIAN EDWARDS

ASH COTTAGE AND CANNON HALL
AT TOTLEY 1978 BRIAN EDWARDS

Brian Edwards.

BUTTS HILL
TOTLEY. 1978.

Next door to Cannon Hall is the
lovely old Ash Cottage once worked
as a farm. Opposite is the Victorian
Moor View built next to the old barns
and stables which formed part of the
Folds Farm. This area was cleared out
to make way for Totley Grange; Butts
Hill was probably part of the 'Monks
Path' from Beauchief Abbey to the
Sheep Grange on Strawberry Lee.

RYECROFT FARM DORE BRYAN EDWARDS 1996

Ryecroft Farm viewed from Ecclesall Woods is approached via a narrow track from Dore Road and the core of the buildings appear to date from the fifteenth century. The Farnsworth family have farmed here since the last century.

This old stone bridge crosses a small brook which feeds that important boundary stream called the Limb Brook in Ecclesall Woods and carries the bridleway from Limb Lane down to Abbeydale Road South. This year the surrounding banks were awash with a magnificent display of bluebells.

BRIDGE IN ECCLESALL WOODS II
BRYAN EDWARDS 1996.

VIEW OVER TOTLEY FROM NEAR MICKLEY LANE   BRIAN EDWARDS 1996.

On Mickley Lane, Ruskin established his unsuccessful St. Georges Farm community. From here there is a fine view over Totley to Roundseats farm and Houndkirk Moor. The Lemont Road houses in the near distance overlook Greenoak Park.

Lemont Road has a fine row of stone built cottages.

LEMONT ROAD TOTLEY
BRIAN EDWARDS 1994

VIEW FROM LANE HEAD, TOTLEY BRIAN EDWARDS 1996.

MOSS ROAD. TOTLEY. BRIAN EDWARDS 1992.

Another view up to Houndkirk can be snatched at Lane Head, Totley where the lane leads down from Baslow Road to Monnybrook. Strawberry Lee Lane can be seen snaking up from Totley Bents.

Moss Road carries up the hill side and becomes impassable to cars at its junction with the equally rough track once known as Deep Hollow Road. Above the junction stands Bole Hill Lodge built in the last century by the Duke of Rutland for his gamekeeper.

I never tire of the splendid walks around Dore and Totley. This track runs from the end of Totley Hall Lane past the strawberry fields and enters into the shade of Gillfield Wood. A short walk away is the bridge over the Totley Brook carrying the path towards Fanshawe Gate.

ON THE EDGE OF GILLFIELD WOOD   BRIAN EDWARDS 1992

MICKLEY LANE
TOTLEY EARLY 1900s
BRIAN EDWARDS 1994

Mickley Lane in the early 1900s had some brick cottages known as Brook Terrace bordering the Totley Brook. Not generally known is that one of the occupants was Harry Brearley the inventor of stainless steel. At that time Harry achieved fame for his performances in forming Ink Blots and Blowing Bubbles

page 42

One cottage didn't avoid the demolition squad. This one on Totley Hall Lane was pushed down to make way for the approach road to the new housing estate behind the Fleur De Lys.

BRIAN EDWARDS 1979

COTTAGE NEXT TO THE FLEUR DE LYS ON TOTLEY
HALL LANE, DEMOLISHED 1978

COTTAGES ON TOWNHEAD ROAD
BRIAN EDWARDS 1996

TROUGH · DORE
VILLAGE
BRIAN EDWARDS 1940.

Dore village has lots of old buildings including this fine pair of houses at Townhead Road. At one time an aqueduct carried water into the village and filled a number of troughs. This particular stone trough is next to Dore Delicatessen..

The Farm' now known as 38 Townhead Road, Dore
served as the Midland Bank from the 1930's to the
1950's. Prior to that it housed the Post Office.

The old infant school on Totley Hall Lane was built in 1827 some 100 years after freeholders asked the Lord of the Manor for permission to enclose common land for the benefit of a school teacher for local children. Sadly the stone tablet is badly flaking and the inscription almost indecipherable.

THE OLD INFANT SCHOOL BUILT 1827
TOTLEY HALL LANE, BRIAN EDWARDS

THE LODGE, TOTLEY HALL LANE 1979 BRIAN EDWARDS.

Standing next door to the infant school is a lodge built in 1887 to serve Totley Hall.

Savage Lane cottages stand opposite the old school entrance in the centre of Dore. Robert Unwin built a house here in 1782 and at one time the cottages were known as Cobblers Row.

The farm buildings at Avenue Farm are the approximate site of a 17th century paper mill which by 1839 had been converted to a scythe forge. Joshua Tyzack bought it and eventually converted it to farm use last century. In 1881 he built the large stone house as a country retreat from his main home in Abbey Lane; his initials are carved above the door.

At the side of Avenue Farm is a Victorian kissing gate, sadly not really needed these days.

VIEW FROM THE OLD SCHOOL - DORE
BRIAN EDWARDS 1995.

TOTLEY FORGE

AVENUE FARM 1995 BRIAN EDWARDS

KISSING GATE AVENUE FARM BRIAN EDWARDS 1996.

THICKWOOD LODGE
OWLER BAR SHEFFIELD
BRIAN EDWARDS 1984 ©

WHITE LODGE NR LONGSHAW   BRIAN EDWARDS 1995

Thickwood Lodge near Owler
Bar and White Lodge near
Longshaw are two examples
of gamekeepers lodges built
in the big shooting party days.

No doubt the grouse shooting parties would retire to the Peacock at Owler Bar. The inn a popular coaching venue, was later a popular target for early motorists. The roads around this area are dotted with interesting mileposts and stones. The cast iron one on Baslow Road marks the half way point between Sheffield and Baslow. The carved stone near the wooden pole shows the boundary between the townships of Holmesfield and Hathersage.

PEACOCK INN OWLER BAR BRIAN EDWARDS 1977 FROM AN OLD PHOTOGRAPH.

BOUNDARY STONE   BRIAN EDWARDS 1995

FLEUR DE LYS TOTLEY 1996 BRIAN EDWARDS.

CROSS SCYTHES, TOTLEY   BRIAN EDWARDS 1978

Long-gone are the blacksmiths and farm buildings (except for a roofless barn) which surrounded the Fleur De Lys at Totley. The newcomer with mock half-timbered and brick construction was built in 1933 and replaced the ancient pub which overlooked what was the village green.

The Cross Scythes at Totley was an extension to an old farm facing onto the village green. Supposedly the first landlord worked in the scythe forge at Hillfoot – hence the pub's name.

DORE MOOR INN 1996 BRIAN EDWARDS

Dore Moor Inn recently refurbished and extended some 180 years
after it opened as a coaching inn on the Dore Turnpike Road. In
common with the Peacock at Owler Bar the Dore Moor was a familiar
Sunday outing venue from Sheffield by the 1850's.

CHURCH STREET DORE BRIAN EDWARDS
FROM AN OLD PHOTOGRAPH

Dore at the turn of the century showing the Hare and Hounds in the centre. Of course many of the older buildings have been demolished to make way for new shops and the pub car park. I have often been asked to copy an old photograph to make reproduction easier and clearer. Very often the task presents a challenge because details on the original are fogged. This one was a particularly good photograph.

Formerly a farm the Cricket Inn was converted to a pub to cater for the tunnel workers many of whom lived in an encampment a couple of hundred yards away. The name was obviously derived from the adjoining pitch the scene of epic battles between Totley and Dore.

The Devonshire Arms was built in the late eighteenth century and stands on the site of a public water trough. Over the years it has been a meeting place for local societies and in the last few years has undergone substantial interior refurbishments although the exterior has changed little.

In 1992 Dore Village Society approached the Brewery with a view to using the old stable to the rear of the Devonshire Arms as a Heritage Centre. The brewery liked the idea so much they renovated the derelict building and used it as an extension to the pub. The village society still has no home for its collection of local historical material.

BARN BEHIND THE DEVONSHIRE ARMS AT DORE
BRIAN EDWARDS 1992

DORE VILLAGE MARCH 1990 BRIAN EDWARDS.

CHRIST CHURCH DORE   BRIAN EDWARDS 1996.

DORE CHURCH 1980 BRIAN EDWARDS.

Until Christ Church was built in 1829, there was only a small chapel of ease to serve both villages. Earlier residents had to make the long trek to their parish church at Dronfield. Christ Church was designed by Richard Furness the schoolmaster. Some gravestones contain references to men who perished during the building of the Totley tunnel. The Church yard is ringed with mature beech trees and there is an attractive Lych Gate built as a memorial.

ST JOHNS CHURCH ABBEYDALE BRIAN EDWARDS 1995

St John's Church, Abbeydale Road South, was consecrated in 1876. The new parish established itself clearly with 6 boundary stones which are still scattered through Dore and Totley. The major part of the building cost was borne by Mr. Roberts who lived nearby at Abbeydale. His friend and successor Ebenezer Hall paid for the building of St. John's Church Rooms in 1893. However during the first world war they were used as a hospital before being taken over by the post office for use as a sorting office.

ST JOHNS ABBEYDALE   BRIAN EDWARDS 1995.

ALL SAINTS CHURCH TOTLEY   BRIAN EDWARDS 1992

Totley had a Methodist chapel off Hillfoot Road since 1848 but amazingly didn't have its own church until 1924. All Saints is hidden away off Totley Hall Lane. Until 1825 Totley had been part of Dronfield Parish and after that time became a township within the parish of Dore.

The Church of the English Martyrs was built in 1964 providing local catholics with a permanent home. Earlier services had been held in the Cross Scythes Hotel.

CHURCH OF THE ENGLISH MARTYRS TOTLEY   BRIAN EDWARDS 1994

page 61

DORE AND TOTLEY UNITED REFORMED CHURCH
BRIAN EDWARDS 1995

HOUSE ON BRINKBURN VALE ROAD
TOTLEY RISE   BRIAN EDWARDS 1995

The Dore and Totley United Reformed Church was opened in 1913 although a group of Baptists, Congregationalists and others had held services in a Dore Road House since 1888. It replaced the 'Tin Tab' an iron building moved from Dore Station in 1908.

One of the Victorian houses in the quiet backwater of Brinkburn Vale Road off Devonshire Road.

The Totley Rise Methodist church school opened in 1931 fronts onto Grove Road and was intended to accommodate 200 Sunday school children.

TOTLEY RISE METHODIST CHURCH SCHOOL   BRIAN EDWARDS 1996.

TOTLEY RISE THE METHODIST CHAPEL C 1911   BRIAN EDWARDS. 1978

QUEEN
VICTORIA ROAD TOTLEY
APPROX. 1967
BRIAN EDWARDS 1990.

LICENSED VICTUALLERS ASYLUM 1994 ABBEYDALE ROAD SOUTH BRIANEDWARDS

The Totley Rise Methodist church was opened 100 years ago (1896) with eight ladies being called on to lay the foundation stone. This view around 1911 shows that the setting was much more tranquil without the dual carriageway.

Queen Victoria Road is a pleasant tree lined street actually in Bradway – it's the other side of Totley Brook. In the 1891 directory it was referred to as Victoria Road.

Now called Woodland View this fine range of buildings, formerly the Licensed Victuallers Asylum, was built in 1878 to replace an earlier one in Grimesthorpe which had been erected in 1853. During the first world war it was used as an auxiliary hospital..

The Monument in front of 'Woodland View' opposite Dore Station, was erected in 1853 in memory of Alderman Thomas Wiley for his magnificent contribution to their asylum by the Victuallers Association.
It was moved from the earlier Grimesthorpe Asylum.

MEMORIAL AT THE LICENSED VICTUALLERS ASYLUM, DORE BRIAN EDWARDS 1995.

ALMSHOUSES BUSHEYWOOD ROAD TOTLEY RISE BRIAN EDWARDS 1995.

ALMS HOUSES
IN MEMORY
OF
ELLEN CARTER
1900.

At the bottom of Bushey Wood Road stand the unassuming Almshouses which were built in 1900 in memory of Ellen Carter. I would be interested to learn more of its beginnings.

Surely everyone in the area refers to the newsagents as Jimmy's. Jim Martins family have worked the shop for many years and will have witnessed the heydays at the Totley Branch Library which occupied the stone building next door. In 1939 the former office and showroom attached to the Electricity Substation was converted to library use which ended when the new one was opened on Baslow Road in 1974.

JIMMYS SHOP TOTLEY RISE BRIAN EDWARDS 1995

THE OLD POST OFFICE ON HILLFOOT ROAD TOTLEY FROM AN OLD PHOTOGRAPH   BRIAN EDWARDS 1994

Standing on the corner of Baslow Road and Hillfoot Road was a small cottage community housing some 50 people.Some years ago most were pulled down, allegedly to make way for a new school entrance which never materialised. Totley lost a number of valuable buildings including this one which was used as a post office for many years.

HOUSE ON BASLOW ROAD ABOVE FLEUR BRIAN EDWARDS 1995

Surely one of the best views in the district must be from the three pairs of brick built houses standing proudly above the Baslow Road.

Half a mile towards Owler Bar stands Totley Brickyard. Bricks have been made in the area for centuries and were used in some of the Totley Tunnel arches.

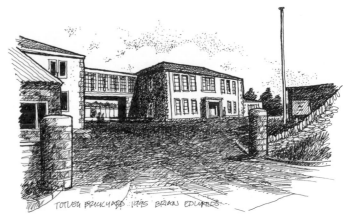

TOTLEY BRICKYARD 1995 BRIAN EDWARDS

DORE DELI   BRIAN EDWARDS 1995.

BRIAN EDWARDS 1995   DORE TUCK SHOP

Despite the formidable presence of the huge shopping developments around Sheffield, some local shops have survived them. The three shops at the top of Main Avenue once served the pre-war development of 'New Totley' as it was then called. Dore 'Deli' has established a fine reputation far beyond the district and Sandy's sweet shop, once Dore Post Office, is a popular venue for pocket money.

TOP OF MAIN AVENUE TOTLEY   BRIAN EDWARDS 1995

THE OLD LOCK UP BASLOW ROAD TOTLEY   BRIAN EDWARDS 1996

The Totley lock-up was situated
behind the stone built terrace below
Totley Post Office. A blank plaque
outside one of the houses indicates
which was the police station manned
by the Derbyshire Constabulary.

ABBEYDALE HALL 1996 BRIAN EDWARDS

Abbeydale Hall was purchased by Sheffield Silversmith John Roberts in 1851 when it was a much smaller residence. He extended the home and gardens and built a grotto (now in disrepair over the railway).

There have been attempts to restore and maintain the gardens in recent years but they do not compare with the glorious days when well known Ebenezer Hall lived there.

The hall has a number of sculptured stone heads – perhaps some one can identify them?

The once proud ornamental gardens have fallen into some disrepair since the hall was taken over as a further education centre. However a trust was established some years ago but sadly the ponds are silted up and the flower beds just do not receive their former attention. A marvellous place to take a lunch time sandwich!

STONE CARVING AT ABBEYDALE HALL (1)
BRIAN EDWARDS 1996

STONE CARVING AT ABBEYDALE
HALL (4) BRIAN EDWARDS 1996

STONE CARVING AT ABBEYDALE
HALL (6) BRIAN EDWARDS 1996.

STONE CARVING AT ABBEYDALE HALL (2)
BRIAN EDWARDS 1996

ABBEYDALE HALL WILD LIFE GARDEN   BRIAN EDWARDS 1996

STONE CARVING AT ABBEYDALE HALL (3)
BRIAN EDWARDS 1996

STONE CARVING AT ABBEYDALE
HALL (5) BRIAN EDWARDS 1996

LODGE TO TOTLEY GRANGE
FROM AN OLD PHOTOGRAPH
BRIAN EDWARDS 1994.

The Lodge to Totley Grange has gone along with the Grange itself and was replaced with a housing estate about 30 years ago.

Only the remains of the gatepost and a summer house standing in someone's back garden remind us of the mansion built by a Sheffield fishmonger in 1875 and fondly referred to as Fish Villa.

HOUSES ON TOTLEY BROOK ROAD BRIAN EDWARDS 1995

TOTLEY BROOK PROBABLY ABOUT 1905   BRIAN EDWARDS 1990

The far end of the old Totley Brook Road once linked up with Grove Road and formed part of the 1876 Totley Brook Estate. That plan was interrupted when the railway approach to Totley Tunnel was driven through the middle. The result was that the road became dog legged and these stone semis stand on the newer section of the road.

At the 'Top End' of the Estate was a reservoir built to supply water to the residents. Remains can still be seen by the footpath through to Hillfoot Road. I suppose geographically speaking this should have been the Old Hay Brook Estate.

1995 BROOK HALL MICKLEY LANE BRIAN EDWARDS

LODGE, MICKLEY LANE TOTLEY BRIAN EDWARDS 1991

Brook Hall and its Lodge overlook Mickley Lane as it climbs towards Dronfield Woodhouse. The earliest record I have is in 1846 when Joseph Ward a 'Coal Owner' lived there. In 1866 it replaced the Cherry Tree Orphanage whilst a new building was constructed nearby.

GATEWAY   DORE ROAD .   BRIAN EDWARDS 1996

These fine gate posts and wrought iron
gates on Dore Road belie the age of the
seemingly ancient house behind, built early
this century.

GROVE ROAD BRIAN EDWARDS 1995

DORE ROAD HOUSES BRIAN EDWARDS '96

In the 1870's, and for the next 20 years or so, Dore and Totley became country retreats for Sheffield businessmen and the opening of the railway increased the Victorian developments. This legacy has provided us with some fine buildings and large mature gardens with many fine trees. Grove Road and Dore Road are just two examples.

Totley Tunnel 1893

DORE STATION 1996 BRIAN EDWARDS.

My book *'Totley and the Tunnel'* is now out of print but copies are available in the library. There is no doubt that the building of the tunnel created the biggest single change to Dore and Totley. Not only did up to 700 navies invade the district for several years but the after effects are clearly visible – although the tunnel entrance is well concealed.

The railway heyday has long gone and we hope for its speedy return. Dore (and Totley) station built in 1872 to serve the London line also provided access to the later Hope Valley line. Nowadays the ticket office, footbridge and central platforms are gone and an Indian restaurant occupies the remaining buildings.

TOTLEY TUNNEL EAST SIGNALBOX
BRIAN EDWARDS 1995   624

SIDINGS TOTLEY RISE 1995 BRIAN EDWARDS

BASLOW ROAD TOTLEY IN 1967   BRIAN EDWARDS 1990

VICTORIAN HOUSES ON ABBEYDALE ROAD SOUTH   BRIAN EDWARDS 1996

Fortunately Abbeydale Road South between Abbeydale and Totley Rise escaped the same fate. Autumn provides a breathtaking 'colourful' route.

page 81

ABBEYDALE ROAD SOUTH AUTUMN 1996   BRIAN EDWARDS

AUTUMN, CAVENDISH AVENUE DORE BRIAN EDWARDS 1996.

Cavendish Avenue in Autumn must be Dore's most splendid visual experience. In 1987 there were reports that these fine horse chestnuts were dying after an application of weed killer prior to pavement laying. Whatever happened, the colourful display was superb this autumn.

page 83

TOWNHEAD ROAD DORE JANUARY 1991   BRIAN EDWARDS.

Townhead Road is another with fine mature
trees and some of the more interesting
buildings in Dore.

MICKLEY LANE TOTLEY
BRIAN EDWARDS 1995.

Mickley Lane has changed from
the days when it was part of the
Greenhill to Stony Middleton
Turnpike. At the top on what is
now Baslow Road stood the
Greenoak Inn and Toll Bar.

Mickley Lane
Brian Edwards 1978

THE JUNCTION OF BASLOW ROAD WITH HILLFOOT ROAD
BRIAN EDWARDS 1990 ©.

LOOKING TOWARDS
LANE HEAD TOTLEY
BRIAN EDWARDS 1992.

The cross roads at Totley once passed across the village green complete with cross, pinfold, stocks and well. The green was surrounded by farms – one became the Cross Scythes Hotel seen here on the right.

The old turnpike was widened and passed out of Totley at Lane Head before rounding Windy Ridge and on up to the Toll House at Owler Bar.

ALDAM ROAD, TOTLEY 1994. BRIAN EDWARDS

GLOVER ROAD FROM MICKLEY LANE   BRIAN EDWARDS 1995.

As new houses settle into a maturing landscape they become attractions in themselves providing that sufficient trees and green spaces remain. Aldam Road and Glover Road are two such examples at Totley.

page 87

FOOTBRIDGE OVER THE
OLD HAY BROOK
BRIAN EDWARDS 1990

STEPS PATH OLD HAY
DORE. BRIAN EDWARDS
1990.

Fortunately the area is blessed with many fine footpaths crossing rivers and streams and climbing hills. Examples from the Old Hay area.

TOWARDS CRICKET INN FROM TOTLEY BENTS 1995
BRIAN EDWARDS

FOOTPATH FROM
GILLFIELD WOOD
B.E. 1995

Happily on hot days our paths take us past a
pub, in this case the Cricket Inn at Totley.

THE KISSING GATE
NEAR AVENUE
FARM DORE
BRIAN EDWARDS
1990

STILE AT OLD HAY DORE
BRIAN EDWARDS 1990

We have a variety of ways of letting people through and
animals in. The Kissing Gate and stone stoops stand as
near neighbours close to Avenue farm.

Walks into the surrounding countryside present us with glimpses of interesting views and buildings.

The Gateway is to Dore Moor House designed by the famous Sir Edward Lutyens in 1906 and in recent years divided up into several dwellings.

As I write Wagg Cottage is for sale. It is set in a small valley by the Redcar Brook.

GATE TO DORE MOOR HOUSE 1995   BRIAN EDWARDS   566

WAGG COTTAGE
BRIAN EDWARDS 1995

THE LANE TO WOODTHORPE BRIAN EDWARDS 1991

MILLDALE CORDWELL VALLEY BRIAN EDWARDS 1995.

DERELICT BARN WITH ELDERBERRY 'ROSE' HORSLEYGATE

JUNE 1992 BRIAN EDWARDS

The Holmesfield area and the Cordwell Valley area within walking distance from Totley. There are lovely lanes, woods, streams, footpaths over fields and staggering views. Three examples from my sketchbook – near Fanshawe Gate, Milldale and Cordwell Valley.

I leave you with a view from the field behind the Fleur De Lys. Just before they developed the area with housing I would come and sit up here sketching. Although Sheffield has sprawled outwards we are still fortunate that a combination of steep hills and valleys combined with lots of huge areas of land has left us with a wealth of trees. All we have to do now is to look after them.

I hope you enjoyed this look at Dore and Totley. Helped by the pens which these days seem hardly ever to be out of my hand, I continue to sketch the area although I now live 15 miles away, I hope to keep sending copies to the *'Totley Independent'* and *'Dore to Door'* magazines for years to come.

BIBLIOGRAPHY

Detailed reading on Dore and Totley can be found in the Local collection and Archives Department, Sheffield City Libraries.

TOTLEY INDEPENDENT:
Available from Totley shops, monthly 15p. Current editors Les and Dorothy Firth, Milldale Road, Totley.

DORE TO DOOR:
Delivered within Dore, Quarterly, Free.Current editor: John Baker, 8 Thornsett Gardens, Dore.

FROM DORE TO DORE:
Some local walks edited by Young & Garland..

DRAWINGS OF HISTORIC TOTLEY:
By Brian Edwards.

TOTLEY AND THE TUNNEL:
By Brian Edwards.

TOTLEY RISE METHODIST CHURCH 1896-1996:
Josie Dunsmore.

WALKS AROUND TOTLEY:
By John Burrows.

I RICHARD FURNESS:
The life and works of a Dore schoolmaster (1791–1857) by Josie Dunsmore.

THE STORY OF METHODISM IN DORE, 1790-1907:
By John Dunstan.

THE STORY OF METHODISM IN TOTLEY:
By John Dunstan.

THE OLD DAYS IN DORE:
Drafted by John Hancock 1896 and edited by Roy Bullen.

'SEKE IN BODY BUT HOLE IN MIND':
A selection of Wills and Inventories of Dore and Totley 1539–1747 edited by David Hey.

EBENEZER HALL THE GRAND OLD MAN OF ABBEYDALE:
By J. Handley.

CHRIST CHURCH, THE PARISH CHURCH OF DORE:
J. Dunstan and L. C. Crowther.

ESSAYS IN THE HISTORY OF DORE IN THE 19th CENTURY:
Extramural Dept. University of Sheffield.

A HISTORY OF DORE AND TOTLEY:
By V. Brelsford.

THE WATER MILLS OF SHEFFIELD:
By W. T. Miller.

THE SHEFFIELD CLARION RAMBLERS HANDBOOK:
Particularly 1920's & 30's.

SHEFFIELDS WOODLANDS HERITAGE:
By Melvyn Jones & Bob Warburton.

TURNPIKE TRAIL:
By Howard Smith.

KING ECGBERT AND THE TREATY OF DORE:
By H. C. Hoffman.

A SHORT HISTORY OF THE RIFLE RANGE AT TOTLEY:
By Stephen Johnson.

THE GUIDE STOOPS OF DERBYSHIRE:
By Howard Smith.

SHEFFIELD AND THE PEAK:
Sketches by Brian Edwards.

CAPTIONS – DORE, TOTLEY & BEYOND
Front Cover: Hall Lane Farm, Totley (See page 34).

ILLUSTRATIONS

PEAK DISTRICT VILLAGES
THE SKETCHES OF BRIAN EDWARDS

A new book to be published in March 1997.